AF449346

BROTHER NERVOSA

Ronald Palmer

Cover Art: Abigail Wamboldt, *Silent Thorn #2*

Designed by Michelle Caraccia

Published 2024 by Barrow Street, Inc.
(501) (c) (3) corporation. All contributions are tax deductible.
Distributed by:
Barrow Street Books
URI English Department, Swan 114
60 Upper College Road
Kingston, RI 02881

Barrow Street Books are also distributed by Small Press Distribution, SPD, 2625 Alcatraz Ave, #514, Berkeley, CA 94705-2702, spd@ spdbooks.org; (510) 524-1668, (800) 869-7553 (Toll-free within the US); amazon.com; Ingram Periodicals Inc., 1240 Heil Quaker Blvd, PO Box 7000, La Vergne, TN 37086-700 (615) 213-3574; and Armadillo & Co., 7310 S. La Cienega Blvd, Inglewood, CA 90302, (310) 693-6061.

Special thanks to the University of Rhode Island English Department and especially the PhD Program in English, 60 Upper College Road, Swan 114, Kingston, RI 02881, (401) 874-5931, which provides valuable in-kind support, including graduate and undergraduate interns.

First Edition

Library of Congress Control Number: 2023951814

ISBN: 978-1-962131-02-5

BROTHER NERVOSA

Ronald Palmer

Barrow Street Press
New York City

[monologues and tantrums]

Ronald Palmer

CONTENTS

Part I: The Blinds

Telekinesis   1
Stroma   4
White Carnations Brighten on a Dimmer Switch   6
Necrotic   11
The Art of the Tantrum   12
The Blinds   13
Make Me Go Viral   15
Traumablind   18
In Blindsite   20
[survivor's guilt]   21
My Mother Blinking in and out of Psycho   23
Outside the Psychiatrist's Office   29
First Fist Fight   30

Part II: Mirror Universe

Derodymus   37
Rave Hinge Between Two Sagittal Heads   38
In the Future We'll Be Born with Two Heads   40
Heathen to Heathen   42
Hysterical Prayer   44
The Next Virus   46
Mirror Neurons / Mirror Universe   47
Voracious Bride   50
Lost Lear   51
Phony Ophelia   52

PART III: BROTHER NERVOSA

Double Hoffman   57
Truth Is a Coyote   60
Voice of the Virus   61
Tress/Passing   63
A Guided Autopsy of Your Phantom   64
Letter to the Ghostself You Meet in Your
      Old Apartment   65
If Desire Is an Imposter   66
Supra-Cerebral Pornographia   67
Portable Oedipal   68
Ode to Graphomania   69
Perversion's Son   70
Manikin: [The Musical]   72
The Octopus Thinks in Mirrors   74
Brother Nervosa   75
Microperas [for Wittgenstein]   77
Self-Portrait with Detachable Ego   85
Echo Chamber   87

NOTES
ACKNOWLEDGMENTS

for Kevin Rolston, my littlebear

Nervosa is the feminine form of the Latin word *nervosus*, which means pertaining to the nerves. Sinewy. Vigorous. Nervous. The psychological addiction to a behavior, belief or habit that effects the body via the nervous system or the mind.

I. The Blinds

Self-portrait with imaginary brother. 1938. Pencil on paper.

—*Willem de Kooning*

Telekinesis

1.

When you are lost
                        this spasm

                        escapes my hands

                        and gathers nerve [overlapping
conversation] with a crowd mulling around the graffitied
wall facing Ocean Beach—

                        talking about two teenage boys
hauled off by the riptide.

                        Two heads full of memories,
the current dragged them fifteen miles out to sea.

[O brother nervosa to be in the throat of a hungry riptide]

                        Blonde rescue surfers return
without the boys with their red surf boards at their sides

                        praying: the mothers wail in
                        film noir—

mothers who imagine the bodies of their boys
careening the paranormal Pacific

                        near the wall of pink graffiti
                        PREVAIL
                        pulls the boys from the waves

returns them, dripping in sea, to the feet of their mothers

invisible hovering drones
place the boys' bodies
breathing again
sobbing in damp sand.

2.

When a part of you is ripped
Out—

there is no script
to recast yourself
in theatrical terms

when I am slow dancing
with your ghost
on the redwood deck
in Inverness, California

your crystal flask is filled
with sunlight

traveling the length
of our reflection
one blur of red
gliding in the sliding glass door

where I was hiding
inside the secret
of your apparent overdose.

I score the boys
in the music of longing

returning from the sea
and standing naked

under the mouth of the full-moon-waves.

I was busy posing
with my boyhood
when a mirror popped
out of my boy
body and said:

Why not pray to the waves?

3.

A pink bud flowers
from a gash in my neck
billowing miniature parachute

        inflating with light
        haunting me at night
        with a high-pitched hiss.

I become a slip-on automaton.

        Cartoonish queen
        as Siamese pawn

prancing around the woods of my own adulthood.

        Projection: A two-headed skeleton
        tap dancing in a 1950s puppet show:
        click-itty clack-itty clack.

        We'll take the check.
        I'm a nervous wreck.

And my erasure is assiduous as dawn.

Stroma

*Like a stealth-jet cloaks itself from radar, cancer cells
cloak themselves within tumors by hiding behind a
dense layer of cellular material known as 'stroma.'*

—*Science Daily*

The son catches his mother's wound—
a baseball thrown

on the other side of the portal
caught with a smack into the palm.

The son wears the wound as a silk dress
stretched across his torso

bone by protruding bone:
pink wound as gown, queen as clown.

He unhinges like a retrovirus
as friends become homeless

in the center of our Milky Way:
an unconsciousness fly-by

blinking in reverse transcription.
Skeletal double—

a mother bursts open: octopus in flight.
I am trailing your wound like a sequel.

Your entrails vibrate—
your brain is electric: sweet fleck

of spit between your lips
saved for the science of hypno-psycho.

I'll wear this mother as a cartoon halo.
I work for the virus now—

thwacked by the bulb of the immaculate.

White Carnations Brighten on a Dimmer Switch

1.

We are surrounded by oaks and birches in a house in
    Northern California.
Looking out a window sipping tea among the wealthy
    beneficiaries of the tech

boom: I'm here hiding inside this notebook to ask:
        what is the sound of my gender when I am silent?

        Do I vibrate on a different wavelength?
        Could an unsighted person hear my difference?

        I ask myself: *how much more time do you need*
        to remake the noir of your new consciousness?

[superimpose a manikin here: dancing in a cloud of
    ghost-voltage]

Maybe you felt safer out there in a new country owing
no one, losing your gun of flesh in the bushes, smoking
found, half-cigarettes stamped out—inhaling the stubbed-
tar-taste staining your tongue wandering the Dutch park
in a childish holding pattern of your own choosing.

        Sometimes I go back into the woods just to watch
          the trees.
        Embrace the turbulence of a mother raccoon
          unfolding herself on a dirt path.
        I observe the living like a home movie projected
          onto pines.

[1970 flashback: a boy sobbing over his home
      haircut in a highchair]

I see my former signature
written in the vines—epoch/apoch
apocrypha / apocryphallic.

Squinting through the cover of holly branches
to see the handsome Peruvian landscaper
      coming toward you.
At the edge of a fence a fly lands on a rain-
      dampened wad of toilet paper
a tourist must have launched over her shoulder.

The moment recasts your flesh into forest
as a yellow finch's branch-hopping fluttering
      above you
is Jungian. At first glance
she is a spy singing the rite of your newly-minted
      husband—

questioning the self:
*is this giant scrim another backdrop for a fake
      practice?*

Lampooning your social double,
two beautiful drunk millennials stumble in furry
      costumes
after the *Bay to Breakers* run, enter Golden Gate
      Park behind the windmill—
I see an orange rabbit and a blue bear giggling
      along a path

joyous in polyester jumpsuits zippered down to
     their bellybuttons
revealing hairy chests, writhing together
in a circle of flowering pink blooms
drooping with the weight of a downpour.

A mother raccoon is no less conundrum.
The bear is on his knees; I watch the rabbit lean back
     and moan
with his hands clenching the bear's blue faux fur.

They are oblivious to the mother racoon
as she searches the lamp glow scripted like cancer
in her genome, she's grunting in the dirt for an
     edible answer—
high stepping with her milky lust and a manicured wig
     of pheromones.
A baby raccoon arrives on the scene.

He does a quick sniff test on the mother
who picks up an abandoned coke can—chugs it
     briefly like a lost sorority girl
before flicking it to hell with her rubbery doll hand
scaring the rabbit and the bear who zip up and tear
     out of there
unraveling speech trailing off. I hear the pitter-patter
     of rain on leaves—
to ward off her hunger she follows the scent of anus
     ingrained in all of us.

[Somewhere the lunar landing is still happening, so
     you hover in reverse.]

You think this is perverse?
Try the end of the universe.

2.

At a recent corporate event they set up VR booths
near the bar and the dance floor where employees try
out various realities: a deep-sea diver, a leader in a
street attack as fighter jets and snipers rain bullets
down on you.

Now here's your chance to be inside the game.

I watch each goggled player monster walk their way to
nowhere, reaching out to touch objects that are only
there if the seer believes in seeing them.

[the next reality will depend on this blindness, this
stronger believing]

Blue, bluer, darker blue just before dusk is done
and the light is bluest behind the oak trees
and you can still make out the alien green of the
    ghost lichen
thousands of silken veils hanging from oak branches
as we walk through a corridor of California Oaks
my love is saying:

there, right there, littebear, that's the perfect blue.

Immunity makes memory work in reverse.
In virtual reality—VR—inoculation is a new faith
falling through the branches
of a California oak
on a hill in Sonoma—

Will they ever get the falling light
accurate enough
to fool our neurons into believing in sight?

Light from the sun setting
enlivens the gauzy veils of lichen
hanging like dread: one thousand
crocheted doilies my grandmother knitted in bed.

Walking hand in hand with my love
through a corridor of Sonoma Oaks shining green: a play
in which we are the deleted scene.

Necrotic

At first your new head will feel unreal
as you cultivate the look of a champion

become a pharma-hydra
selling insulin and HIV prevention.

If you live too long in one stanza
you'll leave it to ruin—

or the story will stall when no one
saves the boys frothing between each wave's tantrum.

Maybe you'll manage to excavate the symptom
shed your second head in the riptide

shed your own consciousness
in what can only be described as a debridement—

The Art of the Tantrum

       Octopus Consciousness—

a tender electricity

       destabilizes a memory.

There's an illegibility around his adolescence

       as he roller-skates

through 1970s sunlight in a tangerine turtleneck.

       [Shark & Boy in Hotel Pool]

The art of the tantrum

       evolves with age

       with *tech-bro*s coding our future

       tonguing acid in micro-doses.

[It's not even real flesh]

Chilling in air conditioning above a California reservoir

       finally to the highest water mark in 2023

parked on the peninsula off Interstate 280 with *Future*

       rapping *Mask Off* on Sirius XM.

A self-surveillance swallows my sonata—not me.

       You're the one arguing with the virus—

No.   *Not this virus:*   *the next virus*

       is already studying us.

The Blinds

Hiking in Inverness on a trail through moss dampness:
    a faery tale
candy-red mushroom decorated with white dots
blooms along our rain-soaked path.

Californian drizzle glazes the cap
so it shines quivering
under a microscope.

All great questions walk in like a riptide.
A spiritual hysteria forever muted.
How perversion mutates inside the manuscript,

turns on inside us as we come upon a hump in the woods:
a cathedral in miniature
then another, a beaver hut five feet from our path—

my love says: *they're blinds.*

Sometimes a word can freeze me in my tracks
pine branches protruding—
a gigantic ready-made Parisian hat.

In a cacophony of identity—
swim out to the country cottage
and visit the hives with me, buzzing among the blinds.

Follow me first: diachronic: synchronic.
Pregnant with vengeance
looping with music, witness a patina sheen

on snakehead lamps lining the paths of Golden Gate Park.
We're sequestered here in the lymph system
of the forest where rain offers a jazz beat

like the Vedic chants we are forever humming in our heads.
Even in my womb of apprehension, silence drags me
into a hunter's blind: *snowblind raceblind sightblind—*

even our love is double-blinded.

We burrow in
and blind ourselves
in the blinds we mine.

Make Me Go Viral

Soul to soul we connect like powder-pink spores
exploding from the pulsing mind of fungi—

> Robotic voice from off stage:
> Make Me Go VIRAL!
> *[yeah… yeah… yeah…]*

In the future we'll auto inject
our immunity
drawn from the furry face of a monkey.
Ambition and antibiotics construct a secret circus
for psychotics.

Using celebrity *Tweets* as news on television
makes it plausible:
will you make me a meme?
Are your pause-able?

> When I'm in the wrong body
> I chat with a charming ghost
> eating room service on a
>   sterile bed
> overlooking the roller coasters
>   of Disney

before the opening ceremony
I'm a giddy sissy in disguise,
awaiting my sales team in suit and tie.
The flashing screens announcing
the PrEP product launch at the national sales meeting—

Make Me Go VIRAL!
Here's Carla in her teens, my
     first girlfriend
with her prayer hands shaking:
shirtless and perfect in her
     Italian torso
folding back the tsunami crashing
over my teenage bed, pleading:
why did you have to be so Gay?

Two ghosts inside the glass lamp
swivel in electric filament
on the bedside table:
they float up and dance the Watusi
above my high school bed
sinking into blue basement cement.

Hotel ghosts transcribe themselves in camouflage.
They speak in a Ginsbergian gibberish, for example:
*Goya's mother's growling in my blind
     spot. Thinks
her theory of Saturn Devouring His
     Son is a
barrage—inside a lucid dream of
     Covid-19.
Hurry, they're de la playa in a
     mirage of osmosis.
A pink tiger in my princess's
     garage—*

With my sex stretched like a dainty pink
     Gucci purse
in mirrored tiles imported from Greece
I am inside the gelatinous witness
in a web of double consciousness

muttering a lingo of a dead fiend—
a twitchy art video in lieu of a sex scene.
Here they come again!
Careening above the flatscreen, the quietest
     ghost sneers:
*Haunting the childhood self is a kind of
     American greed.*

We like to count the dead.
Repeating: *now his T-Cells have telekinesis—*
I draw the black-out curtains.
I leave the ghosts to their breath work.
I repurpose prayer as apology to protect myself
from the phantom hand crawling around inside me.

                    I do push-ups in my hotel room
                    between corporate meetings
                    with the television blaring
                    Mad Money near the window
                    over the seagulls
                    barking above boats
                    anchored fifteen floors below.

With a slippery grip I clap from the floor and float above the
     bed: *clap-clap!*
I smack my knuckles behind my back
     between my shoulder blades
between each push-up, prostrate:
above my head until I levitate—

               my clapping accelerates as my arms blur
               into wings, I raise myself reborn
               and fly into the bathroom clowning in a
                    slippery light.
               Pink and angelic into the full-length mirror.

Traumablind

A curious alien
        brands my organs
hiding in the mucosal lining.

Darting through an ulcer—
chanting with childlike wonder.

If a vaccine's tail is too long
        a virion sheds and leaves a memory
        of itself looping
                                in electric halo
like a recitation—
        a serenade at your blood's doorway

        trundling invisible in triple veils
                                of pink crepuscule,
        dragging elegant entrails:

a petite fashion queen—draped in Alexander McQueen
sleek as a secret

will appear
                        as a bet
against the other intelligence pining
for a flashback:
                        film school 1978:
a red spotted crab scrambling
around in a shallow green
                        tidal pool.

Dormant, Dormmate, Doormat:
in order to escape your hometown
                        arrive in a city without kin

lost as Snow White with cartoon black hair—
shining inside a glass coffin.

In Blindsite

In awe of the way I will wait
catacombic for months
taking notes on my stowaway.

In the middle of my life
sequestered
in a deeper reservoir

in the glandular recesses near my hip.
I pull off Interstate 280
in a grand façade

into the parking lot at Vista Point
within ecstatic Darwinian blight.

[survivor's guilt]

Interviewer [Cis MSM, pronouns he/him/his, voice
    off-camera]:
you were telling me about the current generation,
sometimes coming out in high school or college…

Survivor [Trans Female, pronouns: she/her/hers]: Oh yeah,
well I'm part of the old lady's survivor's guild, the living
witness, carrying all this survivor's guilt because I watched my
generation leave the planet, I feel like I need to be the voice of
the virus, you know, the next one, because now… (takes a sip
from a goblet half full of pinot noir)

Survivor continues:

"They're acting like it's 1978, like POOOF! Four decades fly by
and I mean I'm as sex positive as the rest of them, but it's as if
we did not learn one thing from the first virus, the one that's
still raging, seriously who talks about the one million deaths a
year? I mean globally. Still 36,000 new HIV infections a year
in the United States alone. And me, I'm done with sex parties,
back room sex where you can't see a damn thing, who's sucking
you, who's entering you, I'm trying to tell my younger friends,
homeless kids I meet at The Center, you know I do counseling
down at the LGBTQ center here in the city, and I just say,
[motioning with her hand]: "hey it's happening again, it's
starting all over again,"

and we don't know what's really transpiring, because it's
all invisible of course, maybe it's just dormant, mutating,
who knows, I've had this thing inside me since 1989 and
miraculously I survived because I refused the AZT when my
neighborhood was turning into a morgue right before my eyes.

*I had a nurse friend who told me, you know, how toxic the
first medicines were so I just did the protein shakes and African
herbs and truth be told, some of us survived by going cold
turkey on the sex and drugs until the other meds came out.*

Sometimes I can feel it thinking inside me. No shit!

*And I know we're heading for another disaster, like exuberance
before a market crash, financial, viral, what's the difference?
///because I was in those back rooms and the meat trucks of
the West Side Highway, New York to San Francisco, the piers
huffing amyl nitrite taking God knows how many loads night
after night and I see these blurry kids on Meth and E on the
buses and sleeping hunched over at the bus stops and they're
popping their PrEP and snorting K inside the stalls at the clubs
then the line is out the door at STRUT clinic for their STD
tests and whatever else they're gobbling up in the dark corners of
sex clubs, it's happening all over again, it's no secret, you don't
have to be a genius to see they're re-zippering the sero-sorting
parties, like ten years ago, the advertisements for the POZ
parties, no you don't need to sort out the negatives anymore, it's
just a free for all, like I've never seen before, and sweetie let me
remind you that I'm 68 years young, so you know I've seen a
hell-of-a-lot! I hope we don't have another hellish outbreak like
the first Gay Cancer or GRID as it was in the beginning, but
I have an eerie feeling this next virus is going to be [holds her
skull with both hands] [makes a primal sound of explosion] I
just don't know."*

My Mother Blinking in and out of *Psycho*

Logic is dull.
—Alfred Hitchcock

He is preparing himself
    a blind date:
    sulking in the driver's seat
    of his father's Buick
    1960 my mother is seeing *Psycho*.

She loves sugar, so I know my mother is excited for a sweet treat,
    I see her at the drive-in movies, waiting in line for
        cotton candy,
    behind the big outdoor screen in Greenwich, Connecticut

    on red leather interior
    with a man named Gerald.

    This time she adds a fact: she had a strange premonition:
    something *off kilter.*

    Her friend from nursing school
    set them up

because it's decades before app hook ups and online dating
    before cell phones
help you escape—

she should have told you
                       to carry a rape whistle
                       even a mother
has pepper spray in her pocket book

                              because she should have

mace in her pink purse
because she should have
a switchblade hidden in her dress

                maybe a 45mm handgun in her black bouffant
because she should have
because she should have
                had an Uzi to turn the perp into pink pulp.

                    *

        [fifty years pass]

and you've never heard this part before
a mutation in the viral memory:

she wishes she had called her friend
to pick her up on the dirt road behind the drive-in—

how many times were you eleven
sitting on the 1970s yellow couch
surrounded by red shag rug
and standing on that dirt road with her

until mascara made her a racoon
growling into her tissue
because she should have told someone
now it's your story—
mother you multiply inside me like a virus.

Maybe she could have escaped through the almond shaped rip
in the chain-link fence
behind the giant movie screen

now it's your story for fear
she would be missed among the crowd of teenagers
flirting with coke flavored tongues
in long and large American cars.

She never makes it to the far corner—
her cotton candy in her reflection: she is warping circus-esque
travelling the corridor of shark fin chrome
returning to her rapist back-stepping through the hole in
    the fence.

He is still preparing himself in the Buick
until the moment she blinks into the film replacing Janet Leigh's
blurring black-and-white body under the falling streams
    of water—

my mother blinks back and forth into *Psycho*
screaming in the shower
with her hand raised replacing Janet Leigh's hand
as she closes the shower curtain behind her—
there's my mother cowering in the tub.

[close up on my mother's mouth during the shower scene]
My mother walks out of *Psycho* with Janet Leigh's face on.

[her face mask is shaking like a Snapchat filter
showing the edges of my mother's real face]

Revealing himself as she's bending into the car
ever so elegantly climbing into the front seat
of the Buick's womb-red interior.

Now he leaps into the arms of my mother's slippery
portal where he replaces my mother's face
with Janet Leigh's face doubling down on the big screen

in precision of black and white
Janet Leigh doubling with my mother
blinking out of the Buick back into *Psycho*
then a perfect match: my mother's face floating into place
hovering at the center of the drive-in parking lot.

Each of their hair-doos negate themselves:
both blonde moons, both black moons
bound and fixed with *Aqua-net*
skip-strobing in and out of *Psycho*.

*

Sleepwalking with a mouthful of pink cotton candy
dissolving on her tongue—my mother

knew a fence behind the crowds of teenagers—
dip, duck and run out, but she knew the trouble too
behind the movie screen.

Maybe she could still escape with a painful rip in her sweater
and the first time through the almond shaped rip
a finger of the chain link scratched a reminder in her back
as she imagined escaping to the back road, but to where?
Without a chaperone?

She might hail a porcelain grave in a bathtub
unconsciously ascribing porn to her murderous scream
as the knife comes down again and again under a
    rainwater shower.

Or maybe she'd make it
to a taxi and escape to a gas station
to call her roommate

watching television
at the common room
in her nursing school dorm.

My mother's cowering in the tub behind the theater
where the movie has escaped the screen.
Wet and waiting for the taxi to rescue the date
and pick her up on the dirt road.

Instead, my mother jumps script
and reverts to Janet Leigh thinking on the highway
her eyes darting self-consciously reviewing the events of her day
fretting behind the wheel of a 1950s car
before pulling abruptly off the highway—

mem/or/ator

my mother faking it in the rearview mirror
with movie scenery—fuzzy and filmic—car propped up on
     cement blocks
the stock footage projected on the back wall of the studio—
a world passing by, no wheels, just a phony car with my mother
paralyzed in the back seat under a large, pink hand smearing
     her lipstick

as the infamous violins begin screeching in the shower scene
               [Aiiiiiii! Aiiiiiii! Aiiiiiiiii! Aiiiiiiiii!]
crackles from the bulbous metal speakers
hooked on the edge of the Buick's window
big as the hand of an orangutan.

And because everyone is screaming
no one hears my mother screaming
muffled in the Buick

where sound has memory
scented with butter popcorn
and menthol cigarettes.

You hear the screams
of all the teens
from inside the glass of their 1950s cars

followed by scattered bursts of nervous laughter.

Outside the Psychiatrist's Office

[Outside the psychiatrist's office

where you shove a spicy tuna and avocado roll in your mouth
saturated with soy sauce
where your nose stings with wasabi
and you gulp cold coke
after you sat for thirty minutes and listened like a good manikin
to your favorite psychiatrist
as she told you a story about her life
says that she is planning her ten-year-old daughter's birthday
with her ex-husband who's still her good friend
because this listening   this too is part of your job
and because the sales call never ends
when you become real friends
with your customers selling Cymbalta
selling PrEP Selling Viagra Selling Friendship
and you know she'll write your drug
if you don't act like a pestering drug rep
if you stay inside this comforting performance
of smiling
of listening
of nodding
yes yes: you say, very calmly
chewing the last of the blood bright bluefin tuna sashimi—

then Bluetooth sync illuminates "MOM" on the dashboard of
your company car.]

First Fist Fight

The first fight you ever have is with Linda Rodriguez, a girl
your own age, in the seventh grade; you are neighbors and
therefore more intimately attached, growing up playing
jump rope, hopscotch, blowing pink Bazooka bubbles at the
bus stop, flipping on her backyard trampoline or playing
monopoly on the cool cement floor of her garage. You end up
holding hands that summer with Linda's older sister Kathy,
making out in bulldozers, sending origami love notes up to
her window in a small metal pail, a pail she returns with her
own handwritten notes, you can still see her hanging her long
brown hair out the window looking down at you as she drops
the pail one story dangling on a string.

In summer you and Linda make your hands into tight brown
fists; they are the same color as your tanned faces in sunset
and as she proceeds to punch you, hard in your stomach.
Stunned because you have never been punched, not even by
your own sisters, and because you've never had to truly punch
anyone yet, you never had to make that choice driven by an
immediate surge of panic and dread, but now you're inside—

At first you refuse to counter with a slug of your own, but
then she punches you again: this time in the neck. Her punch
dislodges something feral racing around your childhood self
that warps your sense of neighborly decency, and a sick rage
runs loose inside your body for a split second as the two of
you pant like dogs at the top of her driveway. No one from
either of your families is around to witness so you punch her
back, in the chest, you knock the wind out of her. And as she
runs her fingers through her short black, feathered hair, she's
gasping and so you punch her again while she's weak to let her
know you mean something real is happening between you.

Linda is a tomboy without any sign of womanly breasts yet,
because you both are no older than twelve
and because she punches you back a third, fourth time
and because she punches you so hard you forget what the
    fight is about
and because she knocks the wind out of your body watching
you gasp blinking with tears popping out of her eyes; she is
watching you gasping like a pinned wrestler silently asking:
see how it feels to need air and not get it?

And so it is a fight in slow motion like many events in
one's life the memory of it is also slow, one quarter time in
movement speak, with a neighborhood girl who is perhaps
pissed that you cheated at Monopoly; all those miniature
golden five-hundred-dollar bills hidden in your sock, always
a cheater, always a liar, you wanted so much to be the winner,
or maybe she wants to kiss you now, both of you panting
and crying in her driveway or maybe she sees through you
even now: you're a little arrogant kid the way she caught you
kissing her sister hiding in the bulldozer across the street,
parked in the bottom of the construction site in the black
mineral scented earth, dug out for a pool, snow falling and
clinging to steamy windows, frozen dirt, swarm of snow
under the last street lamp on your dead end—

Now you're offering each other thoughtful pauses between
punches when she feels your punch, her eyes glaze with
tears, you go on like this for years maturing right there in
the morph speed of the driveway brawl, like high-speed
photography, the two of you age fast into your fifties as she
holds her fists defiantly in fight position under her chin and
since you've always had a high empathic response

you begin to cry the kind of cry that vibrates your torso
watching her sobbing because you feel the swarming energy
and know the strength it takes to hold a rage like that
bouncing like a pinball between your lungs packed inside
the skin.

 [Is there a double perversion trapped in the act
of enjoying your own fraudulence?]

        You put the self in the fraudulence
        And drink it all up—

You and Linda standing face-to-face, crying while holding
your ground, four reddish brown childhood fists held in the
air; this is where the love and the fear begin to blur and bind
the shame of losing and the dread of admitting defeat become
undigested meat in the colon.

Under green dusk with a few stars starting to show in space
where they find new planets every day on the end of Sunny
Acres Road.

You reach a level where you can't hear the hero
hiding behind your own voice.

You find your new self so strange
It's as if you can breathe under water.
The dead psychiatrist was right:
when you try on a different head
it's so exhilarating and unfamiliar
it's like breathing underwater.

Put that in your pill
and choke on it.

II.   Mirror Universe

As silent as a mirror is believed…

—Hart Crane ("Legend")

First of all, you are asking a ghost whether he believes in ghosts.
Here the ghost is me; cinema plus psychoanalysis equals the
science of ghosts.

—Jacques Derrida ("The Science of Ghosts")

Derodymus

Careening in cartoonish consciousness
a pink bud
flowers miraculously—
                              blooms from your neck
dangling like a testicle below your left ear.

[A voice from inside the blinds]

Look at you trying to master your chorus of winces.

Twin Adams knocking heads
in bed.

Now you're *Eve-less*—
playing both parts
                              in your canine catharsis.

Blinking inside your self-induced coma
you loop in a memory

                              of your childhood
home you leap through the perverse
portal of your sleep.

Unbutton our species in a nest of snow
composed above the shimmering blue of Lake Tahoe.

Soul-tagged: O my manikin—
proof I still fill with your silences.

Rave Hinge Between Two Sagittal Heads

Our hero is the man with two heads—
        roughhousing with his embryo.

He leaves one head in the trees
swaying with lichen in the breeze.

                I meet him lying
                in the blinds

Passing as tremor. Flashing red knuckles.
Squatting in a business suit shitting on a glossy patch of poison oak.

*I forgive you for everything
        even your nightmares.*

                        [wild-eyed stare
                        followed by heavy breathing
                        a man approaching
                        from behind the tree
                        coming down the dirt path.]

*Crickets breed mirrors
        in surround sound
        in their alien message thrumming in unison—
Dusk descends as a counterfeit species.*

A rumble like an earthquake
on a dimmer switch.

Only sound
for a memory mile
in a secret place in the forest

with the magical light buzzing

in my pocket from a muted incoming text—
[heart emoji from mother]

      I keep forgetting my iPhone
      is always listening—
      running in a mob to Ocean Beach
      as wildfires chew toward us.

Dear self I never agreed
to this drone of the brave: kick-dancing
with furry construction workers in orange vests
and fury tattoos, jock straps, bare-footed

wearing pink rubber arms of the octopus—
suckers with mouths
growling to become you.

I scrub my hair with *Aesop* Everyday Shampoo.
Finger scan the portal listening to *Kids See Ghosts*.
Wrapped in the viper chameleon I've made of myself

spitting venom
in my manikin tantrum.

In the Future Everyone Will Be Born with
Two Heads

The slick suited pharma rep is talking to a woman at the
    front desk;
the medical office gatekeeper.
I hear a patient say:
he looks like that guy on TV selling Viagra, from that movie—
flipping through a magazine in the waiting room.

But now I'm selling PrEP—
Derodymus somnabulent, a double-headed manikin in paralysis
where our grief is briefer
each time we hear the disaster
                repeating itself.

The corporate sales trainer asking: *what is your strongest
    core competency?*

At Facebook headquarters the Lead MD for the TransHealthPod
greets me at the security desk where we get tracking badges and
visitor numbers.
I meet the speaker who's funky with his pink-plastic eyeglasses
and we kiss in front of the young security guard.

[handsome coyote, signs of recovery
trotting along the sidewalk like a prince
saying:
"I know me
coasting in my car, tell my love I'm hiding
in my prefrontal lobe, midnight in Golden Gate Park
your fear stings me in my brain limb."]

Soon coyotes will have one head for virtual reality
and another one for screen functionality.

*

Living in a land of holographia
we finger scroll our days,
we fall in love,
we move to California,
we triple our salaries,
we lose our friends to affordable housing,
we bury our parents,
we camp in the redwoods,
we kiss looking up at Orion
finding us wherever we are
staring at the moon even between pine trees
in our back garden.

Heathen to Heathen

My master chameleon: octopus
        dragging a redheaded anchor
        along the ceiling:

she leaves a smear
        of black ink leaking
        from her fronthole—

traipsing without alarm
        she leaps with an arm
        clinging to a hook in a chandelier:

she swings with suction cups
        that echo her polka-dots:
        a perverse cluster of clots

in the melody of another self-dissection—
        her red legs unlock, release,
        then crawl one by one away from the body.

A savvier signature in lymphocytes—
        an orifice that says:
        fake me a phantom in a mouthful of rain.

Discerning as Orpheus
        yet more *AI* than sentient: a brain
        pulsing inside her own detritus

of translucent sentences—revising her body
        of grief with a bionic wit
        head bowed to the host as enemy

baby teeth clattering in her marrow
        backlit and brightened
        by the wattage of her memory.

Hysterical Prayer

Dear virus
arriving pregnant with vengeance
I am your foreign witness
curdling like a purgatorial friendship—

Looping, driving with music, witness a patina sheen
on snakehead lamps lining the paths of Golden Gate Park:
maybe every disease has a musical solution?

Haunted by the queer diaspora,
deliver me from contagion?

I watch a swarm of starlings in Sonoma
gather like gravity above the lines of grape vines.
The swarm looks like a black tornado
flattening on a hill, morphing into a portal
to another world

where the starlings are seizing in summary,
directionless,
one thousand wings tethered together
as a blueblack mind
that does not know how to proceed with itself.

The swarm churns in sharkish silence
and mimics a virus
                                    cruising the sky for prey.
I see a cloud of black snow stalking
a false winter: a cursive black sentence
hovering in reverse
sketching out a blueprint for a new plague—
before funneling down like an apology into an oak tree.

The black swarm of starlings
          lifts again—

               an epiphany unraveling.
As if dispelling a curse.
As if my mouth is a landmine,

standing on the balcony
I watch the swarm curate the dusk.
I blow blue smoke into the warm July

and I let it ripple through me,
          prayer as apology
then the power quit and we lost television.

The Next Virus

When I was a coyote I carried a man inside me
whispering in a lisp my whole life—
squeamish for fur: flesh-rip, voyeur:

I hid in the seagrass of the dunes
and preened my tail with my teeth.
I watched surfers glide on waves.

I trotted over the Great Highway
like a psychopath.
I smelled of hot tar and brine.

The next virus will arrive in a radio-burst
enter us chanting in childlike wonder
scribbling out tainted copies

made visible in the hovering X-ray
of the next virus
speaking in an army made of mirrors.

The next virus will be more ravenous
than a red octopus: a *snapshot
of my dismantling*

I—orator mesmerize my host
and prey in equal measure.
I stir in my own helium

tapping out a Morse Code message
on your left lung: *antecedent,
I arrive again.*

Mirror Neurons / Mirror Universe

Cocteau loved mirrors and so did Orpheus.
Talking back to the phallus
I see myself

stalking the next virus: alien virion
waiting for my synonym
to rise again.

The virus can build a colony:
enter and fester
make a million mirrors

of itself in a week
after entering a Black Hole
in the blood of its host.

                              [In the aftermath of Fukushima—
                              a two-headed black dolphin
                              can smell a drop of blood
                              through a hundred miles of sea.]

Shot-reverse: the black-gloved
fingers of Orpheus
dip through the mercury mirror

where even scallops have eyes
and supernatural tentacles
go traipsing into portal.

In my prissy elation
I puncture my perversion
prancing within the same body

budding in replication—
a hypothetical chorus
spreads like a mold infestation

across my consciousness.
I am collapsing
into consequence.

*

I remember you slipping
yourself
another morning dose
near the cinnamon-furred herd
roaming around their bison cafeteria
in Golden Gate Park.

We were chatting about a play
that you directed in LA
how your friends were making so much money
at Disney
and you felt like a failure—

*[Loitering like patients
the bison are glazed in mirror
as they trance-chew their
daily stew.]*

And what the dead man meant to me is beyond the point entirely.
I'll say it into the next century:
Derodymus splits the self's sentencing.

[Drug addicts we are ten bison
in reverse
cantering backward in a line
downhill
investigating the periphery of
our pen.]

Then you slap another blue pill
into your mouth: *I'VE HAD IT!*
you growl—

and we burrow back
into our blinds
that kill.

Voracious Bride

Actors invent a voracious bride
to speak in a camouflage.
They yearn

behind a mask
made of parchment:
day-glow orange, day-glow pink

worn by two of the star student-actors—
the leads in *Mr. Burns*,
ACT's Krusty is asking:

what if we speed up the song at the end of this scene?

By summer you're ready to go—

your last four shows illuminate the back windows
facing your night garden
one on fast-forward, another reversing

the way I stalk my shadow
ducking through the almond cut in the fence.
Rattlesnakes curled into each other's groove

Look mom! Two heads!
Should I move to *Joshua Tree?*
Should I move to *Berlin?*

while you are nodding
yes: yes: very calmly
chewing the last of the summer strawberries.

Lost Lear

No one prepares you to greet
the bearded manikin

of yourself—

driving on the highway practicing a story
you tell yourself—

after you leap
through the portal of your sleep

death feels like a film flicker: trauma
as souvenir.

It was a story you were telling yourself
on the highway: you were flying
above sunbaked bird excrement
bright as whiteout
streaking the peaks of Seal Rock.

You are the swarm
of white wings
as you reach the alien realm

floating in a vision of flutter in transition:
ALL REAL GULLS!
recruited to play themselves—

screeching and vicious
in apparition
as a clam shell drops and stops

clattering at the pink hologram of your dead feet.

Phony Ophelia

Light years from my kitchen sink
what would Ophelia think?

The germ of firmness
against her antagonist
as she plagiarized paralysis.

Perhaps she felt her final fall
was a slip of the script—
a suicidal accident?

Trembling in ambient ink
in the dawn of ice
somewhere a pond's still ramping into nowhere—

I toe-tap the frozen surface
at the construction site:
a replica in puddle form
next to Lake Tahoe.

I kneel and hold my head down to the little lake and listen:

ping-tink　　　　　*tink-tink*　　　　　*pink-ping*

lights up a world in me.

It's the one thing we take turns forgetting.
Spinning the gender-wheel and class Roulette—

swallowing the first taste of ejaculate
as a joy-filled, newly trans-Hamlet.

A directorial voice pauses me as I sit
throbbing in my own phony Ophelia.

III. Brother Nervosa

Double Hoffman

1/ Philip Seymour Hoffman: 2001

[monologue as voiceover] "I met Philip Seymour Hoffman in the Chelsea neighborhood of New York City well not really met but grabbed him by the forearm walking down 8th avenue after the gym. I was smoking a skunky joint waltzing in this world of my own making when I saw him talking to a friend in front of Big Cup café; the night after I'd seen him in the Paul Thomas Anderson film *Magnolia*. I felt a connection as if I knew him in real life, so I stepped right between him and his black haired, male companion (who was visibly annoyed that I interrupted but also his face froze in this expression that said: (OH NO A CRAZED FAN IS APPROACHING) but I was in the blurring oblivion of a high person so I grabbed his forearm firm as a wood railing with thick blonde hair, my first thought as I projected the confidence of a senator: *he's taller than I expected, and broader*. I stood my ground and said (close enough to smell his coffee breath) "you are a great actor" with the seriousness of a psychiatrist and he locked eyes with me in that moment when we were animals together, I realized he was studying me, memorizing my earnestness. And even in my high state of being I was glad I made the moment happen rather than obsess about it; wishing years from now that I'd had an interaction with Philip Seymour Hoffman, someone I had admired on the planet so briefly we extinguish, but as I realized the danger (if I held his forearm too long) I broke free and in truth the entire interaction was perhaps seven seconds, but I remember it like a movie. I released my grip and quipped "sorry" and kept walking and smoking and loving being inside my body in New York City all before the twin towers fell into themselves."

2/ Dustin Hoffman: 1995

[monologue as voiceover]:   "Provincetown Massachusetts in 1995 I was working at a clothing store called *SUMO*; they sold *SUMO* shirts with their logo of a green cartoon Japanese sumo wrestler; one night when I was 29 years old, working a summer job the year before I finished a PhD, I was wearing a tight pink cotton half shirt and skirt set, my body, tanned and muscular from running and lifting during the snow storms of lonely gym nights. This one night at SUMO, we are closing the store on July 4th weekend, as the tourists fill the streets, many tourists in the store buying flip flops, and Dustin Hoffman walks in smiling. *I say oh hello we're just getting ready to close* when I realize it's Dustin Hoffman; the tourists begin to huddle outside like kids watching taffy being made, a crowd on the street watching a movie being made, and now I'm in the movie with Dustin Hoffman and the crowd of maybe a hundred people are staring at us through the store windows; we are a secret puppet show: LIVE! They all cup their hands around their eyes at the window, watching me and Dustin Hoffman chatting about summer in Provincetown; he's pretending to look at T-shirts. I'm pretending to count money in the register. When I finish, I hear the manager Kathy call from the back room "OFFER HIM A FREE SUMO SHIRT" because she's too shy to come out and talk to him, strange how the very existence of a famous person makes people nervous, Dustin Hoffman smiles at me and nods. I realize he's pretending to be Dustin Hoffman now, because the mob outside is growing and because they realize it's Dustin Hoffman the actor from *Rain Man* and *Tootsie* inside the store in real life and now he is here as if he's in a movie with me, acting shy. I ask him "Is everyone treating you well?" *yes everyone's been very kind* he says and when I step closer and I realize he is actually standing there looking at T-shirts on the circular rack of clothing, the same man in *The Graduate*, he glances at my legs and says *nice legs* and I say *gee thanks you know, I do what I can*, being a big tan man in a pink mini-skirt I'm naturally comedic, I realize how ridiculous I must look to Dustin Hoffman so I add smiling: *I like to model the new arrivals so people can witness a live manikin at work* and we share a little laugh together. The tourists gradually disperse, and Dustin Hoffman decides it's safe enough to exit the store, joining his own kids on Commercial Street and as he exits, Kathy creeps out of the stock room with a Medium SUMO T-shirt with the green cartoon wrestler on the front and says: *go give him a T-shirt!* I grab the *SUMO* T-shirt and run up to where Dustin Hoffman is walking with his children and I say *Mr. Hoffman, we wanted to offer you a free SUMO T-shirt* and he accepts it saying *oh Thank You* sort of embarrassed and then I say *if it's too small, you can always give it to one of your kids* as I walk back to close SUMO, I hear people saying to each other: *Oh my god did you see? Did you see him?*

Truth Is a Coyote

Truth is a coyote like Truman Capote
courting silence with a whimper
to lure a dog into bloodlust.

A coyote will test the periphery
with a scamper and a hop.

[at the mouth of our drifting universe there's a growl that
     entrances the forest]

They should have known that I would tell all their secrets.

Leave the fur and the carcass to the eucalyptus.
I was simply there to witness.
Turkey vultures big as monkeys: *clack-clack!*

I slow the car and howl out the window.
The coyote turns his body, looks back at me,
like a white comma swirling in darkness.

Let the forest clean what's left of the animal.

Voice of the Virus

We birth like ecstatic tadpoles
                our neurons

vibrating in the calamity
                of our former selves—

heathen to heathen
                our love's in season

did you get your Monkeypox vaccine yet?

I teletype my DNA like a queer paramecium
                flailing in tantrum—

a writer casts a net:
                microscopic suction cups

inside a tangle
                of internal red tentacle—

Lesions too can be silent as Braille.

Whispering in barely audible pop-pop-pops:
                let the mutation begin with me—

coasting the parallel Pacific
                I turn on

like timed greenlights
                along Great Highway

where future mirrors
        will make you switch genders

at 35 miles per hour.

Tress/Passing

Husbanded to delirium

> my body thrown from a seventh story balcony
> in Iraq
> I too am beheaded in Uganda then held up by
> my hair

rounded up like cattle by Chechnyan soldiers
the curse of the perverse

infects everyone here:
I drive to Bolinas to paddle board on the bay and watch
Brando movies.

> hail on the skylights
> hail on the windows

a city of LED is sadistic, a curse
emitting a glow of false light—
even the virus is budding in reverse.

[Now you fester like a secret.]

> [Now you think like a secret.]

A Guided Autopsy of Your Phantom

A guided autopsy of your phantom.
A voice over
as the lights go dim in the academic theater.

Brown moths line the back wall above the cushioned chairs
shivering into double zygote
third eyes stitched into the palms.

Brown moths stitched into the seam of the ceiling—
your shadow walks back to your car
after slipping through the almond shaped cut

in the chain-link fence off the interstates
and worries in the front seat
where a floating red octopus levitates

as you swallow your shadow with chocolate milk.

Letter to the Ghostself You Meet in Your Old Apartment

You say you've never had sex without fearing the virus except
this one time in Amsterdam you were so high on Parisian
hash you let some German guy with a shaved head fuck you
so long and hard it felt more like a fisting in a tiny wooden
hut his cock decoding your childhood in a makeshift army
fantasy built inside the maze of a sex club sweating with your
head pounding against the wooden wall separating the tiny
partitioned rooms with a rush of adrenalin you snapped out
of your benign smiling robot and let men climb up and watch
you over the walls looking down at you to take a tour of pink
holographic skeletons dancing through your soul adrift on
the ceiling saying *so glad we never ruined it* for our fathers,
for our friends, for our friends' Catholic fathers who never
approved of you anyway until you return to your old 10th
Street apartment and buzz the studio on the 6th floor, where
you lived thirty years before you left school for more, more
love and San Francisco, and now your younger self is coming
toward you [here's where the past and the future overlap]
your younger self is thinking —*is it my father?*— as he tilts
his head, studying the future you through the bulletproof
plexiglass, he is almost at the portal door, a quantum
entanglement gone haywire, the portal is closing while the
'future you' disappears right there in the hallway on 10th
Street between 1st and 2nd Avenue.

If Desire Is an Imposter

If desire is an imposter
in both worlds

then maybe intimacy
is the final fetish
that unfurls *you*

burrowing back into your blinds
without a body—

       the boy is skipping
          skip-skip—

       inside the man
          skip-skip.

Skipping,
the boy is.

Supra-Cerebral Pornographia

Gravity is porous
and thinks
like a virus

with each spawning
a salmon hatchery
loses genetic diversity.

We relearn how to survive on dirt.
My mother is still in line at the drive-in movies
waiting to buy pink cotton candy.

Two teenagers in board shorts
stereo-cerebral frolicking on the shore at Ocean Beach
still laughing and throwing sand at each other's torsos

before they decide to wade into the sea
body surf the mind-numbing riptide—
a cerebral scrim drops

a slow injection of freon
into the left hemisphere
revealing the silky squid center of consciousness.

I see the virus
wants to survive
and so do I.

Portable Oedipal

My wit is diseased.
—Hamlet

Flesh-stretch: a final
counter transference

wants the infection to unfold
in slow-motion

hypnotic with two mouths
vying for the same orifice

leaving you a voicemail in 1999
saying:

>*I'm watching a porno,*
>
>*thinking about you—*
>
>*[static. double beat.]*
>
>*[textured hum of a dial tone*

Ode to Graphomania

The mind of fungi invented the Internet
replicating vast tentacles
under a forest of sequoias

while Queer Goya awakened the boy
yawning and facing him on his pillow.

The boy vomited another boy
who crawled from his mouth

[See: R. Crumb   *H. Darger*   *T. Burton—]*

Let me animate him here—

[see animation of boy: climbing from a yawning
                                                    mouth
stretching the lips   as he births himself
climbs down the body   growing larger and hairier as
                                              he descends]

Perversion's Son

Mini-swarms of baby locusts
gush from my fourth orifice
                through my dashboard vent
                they travel over my shoulder

in two tiny green tornados
swaying like lovers above my backseat:
                twin swarms taunting me
                in the rearview mirror

a swarm of green locusts the size of pinky toenails
will suffice—

[Man bracketed by little hives of memories.]

Dear Pacific: what makes the body want to survive?

        If only you could learn to ride waves.
        If only you could walk out into the frothing

waves on an evening at Ocean Beach in San Francisco.
If you pretend that wave riding is easy

pandering to the perverse gland to travel on this ton of sea.

[Pretend you are a person who wakes at 5AM to ride waves.]

You are two versions   of a person
                                a person with perversions
rattling around in your
        telepathy from a double-headed beast—

and yet you share a penis, carnal casino memory lever
        ˙per   /*versions*/   son

surviving like the pulsing double mind of fungi

            the way each new bomb blast
            is orgasmic
            germinating terror—

as you finger your fraudulent self in the bathroom mirror.

Manikin: [The Musical]

Tempo: upbeat, campy, in the voice of Paul Lynde

Black Mittens. Black Kittens. Black Olives.   Black Chickens
In the office kitchen [at the pharmaceutical luncheon]

The doctor is mashing two falafels [green ovals]
Drizzling tahini sauce [speaking of moguls]

He loops the tahini sauce
across both smashed green balls [laughs like a boss]

He's making double Pollacks.
You're thinking: *BULLOCKS!*

Any new drugs in the pipeline?
Where do I sign?

Any new drugs in the pipeline?
How's the family, fine?

Any new drugs in the pipeline?
Everything is mine!

The media controls all the information:
jump through the mirror of hysteria!

Pharmacies control all the medication:
a web-drama looping in terrorama!

I'll only listen to you as long as I can stand
Then disappear with a promise to write your brand.

How's the efficacy, nice?
How's the stock price?

Getting better? Going Higher?
[Doctor, you read me like dark matter.]

Make another lunch date with the front desk.
Sorry, gotta run, this next patient is such a pest.

Where do I sign? Everything's fine!
Where do I sign? Everything's mine!

The Octopus Thinks in Mirrors

Ink me
into your army
of mirrors—

two spirits claiming the same phantoms
        stamped with a meme of memory

writhing in genome
        beneath your skin.

[We were hiking in Inverness, moss dampness, wild mushrooms,
a canopy of birches and pines made a tunnel going downhill and
we came across these strange humps in the woods, cathedrals in
miniature, sculptures of birch and pine with red and black leaves
protruding like beaver huts or squirrel forts: what animal could have
achieved such beautiful artwork like elaborate Parisian hats, ready-
mades left like gifts along the trail?]

And here we begin again
where the *Blinds*

                freeze me in my tracks—

I repeat the word to myself as we hike

as fireworks flash pink hives on our twin skins
my burning manikin.

Brother Nervosa

Brother nervosa   forever in pre-op, prefix
poking your genes

                         in and out
of Caligula's mouth.

    [Ethereal Pink Octopus Drops From Ceiling]
    [Disappears in a flash of pink light, stage right]

There you go strutting through the waiting room
like a fraudulent *Baldwin*.

Fukushima's explosion
and a widening ring of ocean radiation.

    Doctor only sees another pharma-manikin
    lurking in the waiting room with a sales plan freezing
       on his face.

Doctor pacing the length of the table in the lunch room.
Doctor nervous doctor thinking about previous patient
interaction. Doctor wants out of the room.

Doctor wants rep to—
pray for the new virus
quivering in pink glycerin.

You want the doctor
    to give in
    to your hair slicked back
    with Parisian pomade
    to give in

to your teeth bleached white
from gargling with hydrogen peroxide.

You swell into visceral
deer in rigor mortis
frozen blood seals the mouth
tipped toward sky
speeding past the opened animal.

At first the new head would not speak.
Between two sagittal sections of a deer head

where souls drift in and request rebirth
where souls milky as thistle
drift through a Black Hole.

Microperas*

[for Wittgenstein]

**The Indo-Malaysian genus 'Micropera', established by
John Lindley in 1832, recently recorded four new species among
the Orchid flora:*

    i.   *Micropera Mannii*

    ii.   *Micropera Obtusa*

    iii.   *Micropera Pallida*

    iv.   *Micropera Rostrata*

i.   **Micropera Mannii**

Lithophyte, *lithophytic*—I grow out of the armpit
of Foucault.
                    But maybe that's too obvious?

Wondering if consciousness can catch a wound
in Lake Tahoe—with roads recovered in snow

                    when brown moths line the ceiling
                    of your pink hippocampus—
                    [wing-flutter-memory]
                    Is it too late for my canine catharsis?

Gunmetal skin, a chameleon the length of an erection—
but who wants to hear about my identity?
I see two hands raised in the back row.

Climbing over a wad of wet toilet paper
the gun-mental chameleon sprints up the trunk
lurching as it walks out on a branch

of an oak tree, above two men:
one sitting on a stump performing fellatio
on a young Latino in his twenties, smoking a joint.

If we refuse to point to a problem repeating
on a loop, perhaps instead we revel in our bland neurosis?
Our blind psychosis?

Let us celebrate the desire to have sex surrounded by feces.
The *Old-World Lizard* is a non-native species
sauntering toward the chameleon.

When they meet in the middle head-to-head
they're in a territorial fight,
double silver blight unblinking their alien eyes fixed,

their webbed claws scratching the silver bark,
whipping their tails, derodymus mini-T-Rex in silhouette
until one of the lizards tips over like a stiff life-raft and falls

[flailing in slow motion like a Marvel movie]

from the branch in a longshot—
landing on the wide shaft of the man shrouded in smoke
his pink head glossy with saliva.

ii.   **Micropera Obtusa**

The next virus is a landmine smitten in its dungeon:
A stenographer in *cipherotics*.

Gertrude Stein's erotics around repetition
and the cloaking tumor of my Queerness—

delves in like a poison where the musical evening taught us
how to fake ourselves in Catholic Connecticut.

At first glance you'd never know I was the lemon
yellow finch hopping from branch to pine branch: I was a spy.

Un-zippering a question
inside my manikin, I say:

spoil him
like all spoiled boys
want daddy to witness

the disappearing self
orchid-esque

with your pink petals
wilting in reverse.

iii. Micropera Pallida

Try on a homemade head I dare you
to learn how to breathe under water.

Under the weight of this sea of memory
like bipolar Pinocchio

glowing pink-cheeked in the corner
with his wooden mouth muted by lies

and blinking those big dumb eyes
all the way at the end of the universe—

Say, see, this new brain you got here [in noir 1940s gangster]
surrounded by Dark Matter in a toymaker's cottage.

And all that sea traveling within us
reminds me of the Vietnam Vets laughing at the Rorschach

Ink blots projected onto the wall of the ward.
In the 1980s I was eighteen waking at 3AM

we orderlies called it the witching hour
because one of the men, lanky, hairy, in his late thirties,

would wake and walk in a circle near the security desk
urinating on himself and dragging

the stream of urine in a circle, moaning.
He was holding the ghost of a soldier in his arms

missing a limb, they told me when he first arrived
on the Veterans' ward, he couldn't speak:

yet in his dream, he repeats: *we can save him*—
Over and over again.

Which is perhaps why we repeat ourselves—
creating the same cerebral comets

passing straight
overhead to remake the same thoughts in my sky—

like a real boy
wanting for wattage.

iv.   **Micropera Rostrata**

Derodymus looms
Derodymus grooms

        We masturbate in separate rooms
        then make out like teenagers on our
          brown leather couch—

        Holding hands walking Kylie down a
          dark lane surrounded
        by a corridor of snow in Lake Tahoe,
          ten feet high after two storms.

Echo Greco: remembering the gatekeeper saying: *We stopped*
    doing lunches years ago—
When we stopped seeing reps and taking samples.

[OS/Off Stage.   Doctor: What are you pushing now?]

[CS/Center Stage.   Drug Rep: In this scenario I would be
    your cowboy
        talking about PrEP and MSM/ Men Who Have Sex
          With Men / Millennials
Having condomless sex; STIs are through the roof
        so I often have new syphilis cases each week
like a 1970s afro-hero
        riding a Palomino off the coast of genre.
You, with your double-helix, staring at me with a sheepish
    hand and a sandwich
        dangling from my genomic teeth.]

If we are prisoners of our pretending
can we create pleasure inside it?

Self-Portrait with Detachable Ego

Dear Detachable Ego I fly little drones inside myself.
                                Enola Gay: *Little Boy*—

Even heroes need a real job without fear of retribution.
A superior competency of communication.

                                [no audio: indistinct echo]

I chose a performance with my manikin twin,
a Rhesus Macaque harboring a stowaway virus

                                [masquerading as cancer for
                                fifteen years]

Cloaking itself like a *Black Hole*—
nothing escapes the giant pupil.

In the future we find each vacuous gape
tethered to a plague.

Another mutation skips on a record in my head;
my generation's mostly dead

or still in shock— and medicating
daily their queer PTSD
obsessing over data and quota.

                                [nervous nelly hiding behind a
                                shadow inside me]

Derodymus offers a mouth for the voice of the virus
and he reverses me perfectly

under the influence of my own nonsense.

My performance bubbles up as perfume on the surface
up through brackish brown
in a wriggling of panoramic kitsch.

Now off you go galloping
on your new mercy.

Echo Chamber

A film still of the virus
performs this glossy trance on me
where I'm the one swaying in a basement filling with rain.

A mother sprouting out of the crook of my neck—
A tantrum with a cringe-worthy smirk
quivering inside a 3D-printed blood cell.

My American skin cruises my imposter around the internet
with the flawless 3rd Eye of Genet
I am a heathen with a reason—

Conniption. Cacophony: a scratch voice of the virus
with a pink cotton candy wig tasseled
On a Ballerina or Baboon: *O pilot me, my virus.*

A chandelier above your doppelganger
penises hang like diamonds
their tiny purple mouths agape:

are we simply stand-ins for our fathers' fetish?

I binge a lemon meringue pie in my car
catching my rearview reflection I flinch
with clumps of white cream glistening

on the corners of my repulsive American mouth.

Notes

The italicized line *"They should have known that I would tell all their secrets"* in the poem, *"Truth Is a Coyote"* is excerpted from *Truman Capote's Answered Prayers*, an unfinished novel published posthumously by Hamish Hamilton, 1986.

The epigraph for Part II. "Mirror Universe" is a quote from a monologue by Jacques Derrida in which he explains his theory on The Science of Ghosts and is excepted from *Ghost Dance* (1983) by British filmmaker Kenneth McMullen.

The epigraph for the poem, "My Mother Blinking in and out of Psycho" is taken from the following exchange: *"I have a favorite saying to myself,"* Hitchcock tells Truffaut regarding those who complain about his film's implausibility: *"Logic is dull."* This quote is excerpted from the book, *Hitchcock/ Truffaut, The Definitive Study of Alfred Hitchcock* by Francois Truffaut. Simon & Schuster; Revised edition (October 2, 1985).

The epigraph for Part III is excerpted from Maurice Blanchot's book, *The Writing of the Disaster*. Translated by Ann Smock. University of Nebraska Press, 1995.

Acknowledgments

Excerpts from 'White Carnations Brighten on a Dimmer Switch' were included in "The Next Virus," published in KGB Online Literary Review: Issue #6 (Fellow Travelers), edited by Matthew Stadler and Ben Shields.

I am grateful the first readers of these poems who supported my efforts to complete *Brother Nervosa*: Stephanie Young, Jocelyn Saidenberg, Chet Wiener, Camille Roy, Pam Martin, Syd Staiti, Yedda Morrison, Eric Sneathen, Samantha Giles, Christian Nagler, and Rebeca Bollinger.

Thank you to Peter Nickowitz, C. Dale Young, Faith Adiele, Andrea Greenberg, and Drew Cushing who motivated me during a critical point in the editing process when I was ready to give up on this manuscript.

I am grateful for Peter Covino for championing *Brother Nervosa*. Thank you to Shannon Carson and Rachel Rothenberg and everyone on the editorial board at Barrow Street Press for believing in this manuscript. You have my deepest appreciation for everything you do to promote poets and writers.

To my parents, Ron Sr. and Linda, and my sisters, Lisa and Yvonne: thank you for teaching me how to be a devoted son and a better brother.

Thank you to my brave husband, Kevin Rolston, for loving me, inspiring me, and showing me, by your own example, how to transform.

Photo Credit: Ben Krantz Studio

Ronald Palmer was raised in Bethel, Connecticut. He received degrees in English from the University of New Hampshire (B.A.), New York University (M.A.) and Binghamton University (Ph.D.). He has taught Literature and Creative Writing at Framingham State University, in Framingham, Massachusetts as well as New York University and The New School in New York City. He is the author of a first poetry collection, *Logicalogics* (Soft Skull Press) and a novel, *Prick Queasy* (Publication Studio, Fellow Travelers Series). Palmer received a postdoctoral grant to work as a writer-in-residence at The Jan van Eyck Akademie in Maastricht, Netherlands. He returned to the United States in 2000 and began a career in biotechnology sales. Many of the poems in *Brother Nervosa* were written while working for Pfizer, Lilly, Teva, Gilead Sciences, Biogen, and GlaxoSmithKline (GSK). He lives in the Richmond District of San Francisco near Golden Gate Park with his husband, Kevin Rolston, and their magical Aussie Shephard, Kylie Fantastic.

BARROW STREET POETRY

Brother Nervosa
Ronald Palmer 2024

The Fire Road
Nicholas Yingling 2024

Close Red Water
Emma Aylor 2023

Fanling in October
Pui Ying Wong 2023

Landscape with Missing River
Joni Wallace 2023

Down Low and Lowdown...
Timothy Liu 2023

*the archive is all
in present tense*
Elizabeth Hoover 2022

Person, Perceived Girl
A.A. Vincent 2022

Frank Dark
Stephen Massimilla 2022

Liar
Jessica Cuello 2021

*On the Verge of Something Bright
and Good*
Derek Pollard 2021

*The Little Book of
No Consolation*
Becka Mara McKay 2021

Shoreditch
Miguel Murphy 2021

Hey Y'all Watch This
Chris Hayes 2020

Uses of My Body
Simone Savannah 2020

Vortex Street
Page Hill Starzinger 2020

*Exorcism Lessons
in the Heartland*
Cara Dees 2019

American Selfie
Curtis Bauer 2019

Hold Sway
Sally Ball 2019

Green Target
Tina Barr 2018

Luminous Debris: New &
Selected Legerdemain
Timothy Liu 2018

We Step into the Sea: New and
Selected Poems
Claudia Keelan 2018

Adorable Airport
Jacqueline Lyons 2018

Whiskey, X-ray, Yankee
Dara-Lyn Shrager 2018

For the Fire from the Straw
Heidi Lynn Nilsson 2017

Alma Almanac
Sarah Ann Winn 2017

A Dangling House
Maeve Kinkead 2017

Noon until Night
Richard Hoffman 2017

Kingdom Come Radio Show
Joni Wallace 2016

In Which I Play the Run Away
Rochelle Hurt 2016

The Dear Remote
Nearness of You
Danielle Legros Georges 2016

Detainee
Miguel Murphy 2016

Our Emotions Get Carried Away
Beyond Us
Danielle Cadena Deulen 2015

Radioland
Lesley Wheeler 2015

Tributary
Kevin McLellan 2015

Horse Medicine
Doug Anderson 2015

This Version of Earth
Soraya Shalforoosh 2014

Unions
Alfred Corn 2014

O, Heart
Claudia Keelan 2014

Last Psalm at Sea Level
Meg Day 2014

Vestigial
Page Hill Starzinger 2013

You Have to Laugh:
New + Selected Poems
Mairéad Byrne 2013

Wreck Me
Sally Ball 2013

Blight, Blight, Blight,
Ray of Hope
Frank Montesonti 2012

Self-evident
Scott Hightower 2012

Emblem
Richard Hoffman 2011

Mechanical Fireflies
Doug Ramspeck 2011

Warranty in Zulu
Matthew Gavin Frank 2010

Heterotopia
Lesley Wheeler 2010

This Noisy Egg
Nicole Walker 2010

Black Leapt In
Chris Forhan 2009

Boy with Flowers
Ely Shipley 2008

Gold Star Road
Richard Hoffman 2007

Hidden Sequel
Stan Sanvel Rubin 2006

Annus Mirabilis
Sally Ball 2005

A Hat on the Bed
Christine Scanlon 2004

Hiatus
Evelyn Reilly 2004
3.14159+
Lois Hirshkowitz 2004

Selah
Joshua Corey 2003